Opinion Disclaimer

The views and opinions expressed herein are those of the author and do not necessarily reflect the official policy or position, nor is it intended to make medical claims of any kind nor is it intended to discourage treatment or medications. Any content provided by the author is not intended to malign any religion, ethnic group, club, organization, company, individual or anyone or anything.

For order/reprint requests contact

202.241.1542 or lynn@livinglarger.life

12 STEPS FOR CLIMBING OUT OF THE

DARK PLACE

by Lynn Gardner

INTRODUCTION

I'm not a psychiatrist, phycologist, counselor or pastor. I don't write prescriptions for medications and I don't take them either. This book does not address mental illness or chronic chemical imbalances. I recognize that sometimes the *dark place* is only manageable with prescription medications, but I honestly don't believe that's the case for most people.

This this book is not intended to discourage you from seeking treatment or medications of any kind. It's <u>your</u> journey, and only <u>you</u> can decide what's best for your life.

Perhaps someone has shared this book with you in hopes of helping you climb out of the dark place and you're only reading because you promised them you would.

Maybe you're just curious about a concept that you think is lame for dealing with your darkness.

You might even be reading in hopes of finding answers for someone you love.

 Whatever the reason, I'm glad you're here and I pray you find answers to help you along in climbing out of the *dark place*.

I don't believe in coincidence and it's no mistake that you've found your way here.

I hope you'll consider the possibilities with an open mind.

You just never know when a golden nugget will come along that has the potential to change your life forever.

I'm hoping this is yours.

FIRST THINGS FIRST

If you were to poll people who are in bondage to addiction…whether it's alcohol, drugs, gambling, pornography or food…and you asked them if they could take a pill to conquer their addiction, don't you think they would? You better believe they would! But it's not that simple for addiction and its not that simple for depression either!

We don't conquer the things that have taken control of our lives…the things that have turned our lives upside down…the ones that hold us "hostage" … with an easy-fix prescription! It simply doesn't work that way.

It takes hard work to climb out of the dark place the same as it does to overcome addiction!

Do you really think that someone addicted to heroin has an easier time of it than you do, or that their journey is any easier to walk than yours is? Think again! Addiction is physically, mentally, emotionally and spiritually destructive and it's the worst kind of thing to overcome - and yet, it has been statistically proven over decades of study that an addict is more likely to reach long-lasting recovery by following a simple "12 Step Program" over any other treatment plan out there.

Why is that? More than therapy, more than any DIY strategy, more than retreats that focus on addiction, more than hypnosis or acupuncture, time and time again the step-by-step program prevails hands-down!

Could it be that when we're faced with problems that feel insurmountable that we have a better chance of "recovery" if we **break it down into bite-sized pieces?**

By now you might be rolling your eyes over the idea that a simple 12 Step Program could help you, and you're probably not happy with me for simplifying your problem. I don't know what I'm talking about, right? WRONG!

I've been in that dark place.

I know what it is to lose hope.

I know what it feels like to have no will to live.

I know what it is to lose the strength to go on.

I know what it means to believe the world would be better off without me!

The only difference between you and me is that I learned to fight back, and I conquered the dark place before it *completely* devoured me…**one bite-sized piece at a time**.

If I can do it, then you can do it too! One step at a time.

YOU'RE NOT THE ONLY ONE!

You may feel like you're the only one suffering in the dark place but you're not the only one by far! In addition to close friends, family, co-workers and strangers you pass on the street, there are plenty of successful, high profile, influential people who ended up in that dark place too. How did they manage not only to "function" in the dark place, but <u>to EXCEL in the dark place too</u>?

First, they tapped into the power of God. Everything on the planet and everyone that has ever lived KNOWS that there is One more powerful than they are!

There **is** a Higher Power – I call Him God, the Father of Jesus Christ – but even those who don't share my faith STILL understand that something exists that is more powerful than they are!

When put to the test, every living creature will cry out to that Higher Power!

Let's face it - you either believe that SOMETHING more powerful than you exists - OR you voluntarily surrender all the power to the dark place to control your life forever! Depression has no power of its own – we *surrender* the power to it instead!

It all comes down to this - will you surrender the power to God to help you find your joy again OR will you surrender your power over to depression that will rob you of everything good for the rest of your life?

The choice is yours.

Acknowledging God, and His power to see us through, was the saving grace (in more ways than one) for plenty of people throughout history…successful, intelligent, high profile, influential people that suffered through the dark place without letting the dark place dictate their future!

Let's take a look at some of the most influential people of all times…straight from the Bible itself:

DAVID

David was troubled and battled deep despair. In the Psalms David writes of his anguish, loneliness, fear of the enemy, his heart-cry over sin, and the guilt he struggled with because of it. We also see his overwhelming grief in the loss of his son in 2 Samuel 12:15-23 and 18:33.

David's **honesty with his own weaknesses** gives hope to those of us who have struggled with overwhelming depression.

"My guilt has overwhelmed me like a burden too heavy to bear." - Psalm 38:4

Have you ever felt that your burden was too heavy to bear?

I have!

You have!

Even David, the "man after God's own heart" did!

"Why are you downcast, O my soul? Why so disturbed within me? Put your hope in God for I will yet praise him, my Savior and my God" Psalm 42:11

Can you feel David's despair in his words? He's talking to himself like so many of us do and he wants to know *why his soul is downcast and why his spirit is disturbed!* David needed to understand with his mind what his heart felt!

Haven't you asked yourself the same questions in different words?

Don't you long to understand with your mind what your heart feels when you're in the dark place? Of course, you do! It's miserable in the dark place and if we could wish our way out of there, we would!

Haven't you gone a step farther by giving yourself a good lecture for why you're in the dark place when everybody around you is telling you *to get over it*?

There's is one significant difference between David and how most of us cope…David finishes his sentence by proclaiming that he **will STILL praise his Savior – despite his downcast heart!**

Do you still praise your "higher power" ESPECIALLY when you find yourself in the dark place? Your "higher power" is THE ONLY thing that will see you through and pull you out of the darkness! Without God, we ARE powerless! Learn from David – the expert on despair…. praise your "higher power" through it all!

THANK YOU FOR GIVING ME A NEW DAY

THANK YOU FOR LIFTING MY SPIRIT

THANK YOU FOR SEEING ME THROUGH

THANK YOU FOR MY FAMILY

THANK YOU FOR MY HEALTH

THANK YOU FOR MY HOME

THANK YOU FOR MY JOB

THANK YOU FOR ALL THAT YOU DO FOR ME!

Never, EVER underestimate the power of an attitude of gratitude! You might just be surprised at how much lighter you feel just by doing what David did…<u>continue to praise your "higher power" no matter what – and be grateful for God ESPECIALLY in the pit of darkness!</u>

There is TREMENDOUS peace in knowing that God is always there and that He promises to see us through any trial we face.

There is HOPE when we believe!

Is it any wonder that the very first step in the Alcoholics Anonymous 12 Step Program for recovery is to ADMIT that we are **POWERLESS**?   Most people are introduced to the 12 Step Program long after other things have failed. They've battled and battled and lost every time. Why? Because they fooled themselves into believing that they could do it on their own. Much of the success of this program comes down to ADMITTING that you alone cannot overcome…and that's where the Higher Power comes in!

You might have people in your life that have judged you for being in the dark place, but God never will. God understands where you are, and **He wants to help you climb out!**

Time and time again God reached down to comfort one of His own in their darkest hour, and **He'll do the same for you!**

God didn't lecture them, and He didn't tell them to "get over it."

He didn't threaten them or issues ultimatums.

 He didn't judge them.

He didn't spit out advice and insults…although HE has every right to do all those things!

Instead, He extends *compassion* over and over again and He promises to "take you by the right hand and lead you." God is the ultimate promise keeper!

ELIJAH

Elijah was discouraged, weary, and afraid. After being eye-witness to one of the greatest spiritual victories the world has ever known, this mighty man of God was overwhelmed by fear and he ran for his life like a wussie - far away from the threats of Queen Jezebel (who ordered that he be beheaded). Elijah watched as God miraculously destroyed 400 false prophets, and at a time when Elijah should have been flying high…he fled to the desert defeated and worn out…and he surrendered to the dark place.

"I have had enough Lord, he said. Take my life, I am not better than my ancestors." 1 Kings 19:4

Instead of being encouraged by his recent victory, Elijah was DIScouraged, and he hit that dark place faster than we can say "amen."

How many times has someone you love told you to "snap out of it" as they reminded you of all the reasons YOU have for being happy?

Elijah had reason to be happy too, but circumstances overwhelmed that great Prophet the same as circumstances have the potential to overwhelm you and me!

We can learn a lot from Elijah. If a mighty man of God can slip into that dark place in the aftermath of a major victory, then **it can happen to any one of us- even when things are good!**

What did Elijah do when he sank into the dark place?

He cried out the Living God and <u>confessed</u> his downcast heart, and when he did, God tended to his brokenness right away, *in every way.*

I Kings 19

Elijah was afraid and ran for his life. When he came to Beersheba in Judah, he left his servant there, while he himself went a day's journey into the wilderness. He came to a broom bush, sat down under it and <u>prayed that he might die.</u> "I have had enough, Lord," he said. "Take my

God KNEW Elijah was weary and He made sure to tend to his weak physical state FIRST to ready him for the spiritual journey ahead. Now THAT'S a compassionate "higher power!"

As surely as God sent help to Elijah, He will send help to you and me too! When we cry out to the ONLY One with the Power to pull us out of the dark place, **HE HEARS US!**

Jonah was angry and wanted to run away. After God called Jonah to go to Nineveh to preach to the people there, he fled as far away as could. He didn't want to obey God. He didn't want to preach there. Jonah didn't believe the people of Nineveh deserved the mercy of God and He didn't want to go there to warn them with the message God told him to share. So, he rebelled instead. Jonah tried to run away from God by seeking refuge on a ship headed for a place far away from Nineveh, but you can't outsmart, or outrun God.

A massive storm rocked that ship and Jonah was tossed overboard into the raging sea and swallowed up by a giant fish.

He spent 3 days in the belly of that giant fish until He surrendered his will and pleaded for mercy. **God gave Jonah a second chance** and Jonah reluctantly preached the message – word for word – to the people of Nineveh. They embraced the message and turned to God, and thousands of lives were saved as a result. I'm sure God was happy with the results but Jonah sure wasn't. Instead of rejoicing, Jonah got angry.

1 Kings 19

"Now O Lord, take away my life, for it is better for me to die than to live." Jonah 4:3

Even after God <u>reached out to Jonah again</u> with great compassion, providing a little shade from the sun, Jonah STILL responded with

"I am angry enough to die." Jonah 4:9

Before you jump-the-gun to judge Jonah, take a realistic look at your own attitude first.

Is it anger that keeps you from climbing out of the dark place?

Do you think life is unfair and that God doesn't know what He's doing when it comes to you and what *you think* you deserve?

Jonah wasn't just angry over being asked to do something he didn't want to do, he was *consumed with self-centered thoughts*. He fussed and whined about the unfairness of God and it almost cost him his life. It was his focus on what HE perceived to be unfairness that sunk him into despair, and even the compassion of a loving God couldn't soften him.

Have you found yourself laser-focused on your own circumstances and stomping like a 2-year-old because you think your life should be one way and it's not? If you've been in the dark place, I'm pretty sure you have!

Even when Jonah was in the dark place (as a result of his own selfish heart) God still extended compassion to him in hopes of pulling Jonah out. But Jonah refused because having his own way was much more of a priority for him than getting out of the dark place!

Do you see yourself in Jonah? Are you lingering in the dark place because you think your life *should be different* than it is?

Life happens to ALL of us and it has no place for pity-parties.

You will NEVER find joy or peace if you determine to focus on what you THINK you deserve instead of what you <u>already have.</u>

None of us can totally control our circumstances, but we CAN control how we deal with them. Attitude is 99% of the battle!

Jonah threw in the towel and ignored the God so willing to help him. Is that what you're doing too? If so, and I say this as kindly as I can, **you are the reason you're in the dark place**

Stop looking at your circumstances through the eyes of someone who believes they "deserve" this or that, and start looking at them as something you can conquer or overcome…with the help of the God of all circumstances.

It all comes back to whether or not you believe that there is a God much bigger than your circumstances. He will extend compassion to you as surely as He did to Jonah if you'll humble yourself and ask for His help!

JOB

Job suffered through great loss, devastation, and physical illness. This righteous man of God literally lost everything within a <u>matter of minutes</u>…his children, his health, and his wealth….GONE within minutes! So great was his suffering and tragedy that even his wife said, *"Are you still holding on to your integrity? Curse God and die!"* <u>Job 2:9</u>

You think you've got problems? I doubt anybody reading this book has ever had everything (but a nagging spouse) taken from them within a matter of minutes! Job was "the most righteous man alive," and although he maintained his faithfulness to God, he still struggled deeply through the clutches of emotional and physical pain and he found himself in the dark place wishing he'd never been born.

"Why did I not perish at birth, and die as I came from the womb?" Job 3:11

"I have no peace, no quietness, I have no rest, but only turmoil." Job 3:26

"I loathe my very life; therefore, I will give free rein to my complaint and speak out in the bitterness of my soul." Job 10:1

Have you ever found yourself wishing you'd never been born? Probably so, but with *circumstances far less devastating* than what poor Job endured.

Even though Job was "the most righteous" man on the planet at the time, he STILL had to suffer through unimaginable circumstances the likes of which you and I couldn't never bear!

Life happens to all of us. None of us get to breeze through life without problems and heartbreaks and sometimes we wish we'd never been born! When you read Job's words it's hard to imagine that he could have even a glimmer of hope for the future.

What does a guy do when he has lost *everything*...his children...his health...his wealth...all in a matter of minutes? He turns to God...his only hope...**his "Higher Power."**

Job didn't have a pity-party and he never said, "why me?" He never stopped praising God. Job spent a whole lot more time reflecting on how he could be more pleasing to God than how God could be more pleasing to Him! Job didn't question the Hand of God!

In the end, God restored everything to Job...in fact, he gave Job a "double measure" of everything he lost.

Job was pulled out of the dark place, his life was restored, and he went on to live a beautiful life despite the losses.

Do you spend more time than you ought to wondering WHY you have the life you have or WHY your circumstances are "impossible" for you to endure? Sometimes the answer is…"It just is"

If anybody had the justification to woller in self-pity and question the unfairness of God, it would be Job. But Job understood who was in control and he refused to quit loving (and praising) Him; and because of that, his life was restored in double measure in the end.

It serves no good purpose to wonder why, or to woller in self-pity over the life you wish you had (or don't have). The only way out of the dark place is to remember **that life happens to all of us** AND that there is a God out there longing to pull us out of the dark place so that He can restore our lives too!

Before you let yourself get caught up in thinking *"but nobody knows what my life is like"* I'll agree with you and save you the trouble.

I don't know what your life is like, and I'm sure I wouldn't want your troubles. But you don't what my life is like either and believe me you wouldn't want to trade places if you could.

None of us can begin to imagine what Job felt like and we sure wouldn't want his life because of it. **The point is, you get an imperfect life just like everybody else and what you make of it is the difference between joy and torment.**

If you want to climb out of the dark place like Job did, stop focusing on your imperfect life. **You can't do anything about perfecting your imperfect life UNLESS you get out of the dark place!**

Haven't you suffered long enough?

Own it, reject it or change it. It's refusing to do any of those things that will rob you of your peace and keep you in the dark place all the days of your life. If Job had done that with his super-sized problems, he would never have found his way to the victory that we still read about today.

Be like Job.

There are plenty of other famous people that have had firsthand experience with the dark place just like you have

Each one of these people also lived *extraordinary lives* despite their inclination toward depression that was apparently big enough or bad enough to be written about years after their passing!

Do you recognize any of these names?

Abraham Lincoln

Nikola Tesla

Vincent van Gogh

Wolfgang Amadeus Mozart

Charles Darwin

Michelangelo

Charles Dickens

Julius Caesar

Napoleon Bonaparte

Ludwig van Beethoven

Winston Churchill

Ernest Hemingway

Isaac Newton

Virginia Woolf

J.C. Penney

Abraham Lincoln and J.C. Penney are known to have been devout Christians and we have read their firsthand account of how God pulled them out of the dark place and set them back on course to live an extraordinary life despite the dark place challenges!

"I am driven to my knees by the conviction that I have nowhere else to go." **Abraham Lincoln**

But what about all the others that may or may not have leaned on the power of God?

How did they find their way out of the dark place and accomplish such greatness?

We don't know for sure, but I believe the biggest factor is that they each had **a purpose...a dream...a vision much** bigger than their depression, and it was that dream that gave them the strength to persevere!

The Bible says *"hope deferred makes the heart sick"* so it stands to reason that when we quit dreaming, we quit having anything to look forward to, and THAT'S when the heart becomes **sick.** But that verse doesn't end there – it goes on to say, *"but a longing fulfilled is a tree of life!"*

Because the dream was bigger than their depression, these guys understood how to face their enemy (the dark place) head-on instead of embracing it (depression) as part of who they were.

They learned how to cope without the benefit of Prozac (or any other antidepressants), and they clearly didn't spend most of their lives in bed with the shades drawn and the covers pulled over their head. Their success is the biggest indicator that they didn't let that happen.

I think they had coping skills that empowered them to REJECT the inclination toward the dark place out of pure determination, never allowing it to take full control of their lives. No doubt it hindered their quality of life occasionally, but they were overcomers and they were determined dreamers!

Have you given up on your dreams?

Is it possible that you quit dreaming and then found your way to the dark place INSTEAD of the dark place being the cause for you to stop dreaming? I don't think it's possible…I think it's **probable**!

Is there something you dreamed of doing but you quit believing in the possibilities? Don't you know that EVERYBODY has doubts and set-backs in the journey called life?

Quitting is a choice.

Determination is the difference maker!

If you've quit dreaming…if you have no vision…if you won't *allow* yourself to look into the future with hope – then you can't (or won't) climb out of the dark place! **You were BORN with a purpose in mind!**

Do you embrace your depression as a part of who you are? Have you "accepted" it as your norm – the way you'll always be…just the way you are…the burden you must carry…the reason you don't find happiness…the excuse for not being productive?

Never, EVER embrace the dark place or accept it as your norm.

When we surrender the fight and accept something (like depression), we give it permission to take up residency in our lives. This is true for any struggle from addiction to depression.

Nobody can overcome the struggles by embracing them. The dark place IS your enemy and it comes from an even darker place that has an endless supply of discouragement and self-doubt to dump on you anytime you're ready.

Your feelings are *real*.

Your depression is *real*.

The dark place is a *real* place, but it NEVER has to become who you are or dictate your destiny. It's NOT your DNA.

HOPE IN A BOTTLE

Once again, **I AM NOT** against medication if it is necessary to address mental illness or chemical imbalances and my words are NOT INTENDED to discourage you from seeking medical advice and/or prescribed medication! In fact, I'm thankful there is help for those people with chemical imbalances and I'm glad many of them find their way to "sanity" just by addressing the imbalances with medication. <u>Imbalances are real, they are serious and most of the time the ONLY way to address them IS with the proper medications.</u>

Mental illness/chemical imbalances are an entirely different story than the dark place we're addressing here, and no amount of "coping skills" can help most people suffering with those physical issues.

As for all the rest of us, **a pill isn't the long-term solution for climbing out of (and staying out of) the dark place.**

A pill for depression will mask the underlying problem as surely as a pill will mask the symptoms of any other ailment. The problem still lingers in the background – it's just softened by medication.

There is no cure for any disease on the planet, and a pill doesn't exist that will change your circumstances or fix your depression. Yet, that's the first thing most people reach for when they look for help to cope with life.

Getting temporary relief when life has become too hard deal with is one thing…and it's a good thing! But taking an antidepressant for the rest of your life comes with a price - and it makes no sense at all.

I wonder if the "famous" people I've listed would have ever accomplished their greatness had they taken a pill to mask the symptoms instead of learning to press-on despite the dark place?

Prescriptions for antidepressants rose by 65% between 1999 and 2014 and the numbers climb higher every day!

What changed?

Why are so many MORE people being told they're in need of antidepressants?

What' is the cause for the climb?

Could it be that we no longer know how to cope?

Could it be that we're being dragged down by all the "darkness" in the world around us?

If there an underlying medical condition?

Could it all come down to "supply and demand" because we'd much rather take a pill to fix the problem than to put forth the effort to learn how to cope?

I'm not sure if that's the case with antidepressants or not, but I DO know that's a common problem in the world of health today! We refuse to put in the effort it takes to be healthy - and we opt for a pill to mask the symptoms every single time. With that in mind, COULD it be that this mindset carries over to the dark place too?

Instead of offering encouragement, prescribing a full medical work-up, or prescribing counseling FIRST, the medical community would much rather write a prescription because it's *the gift that keeps on giving for you and for them!*

Unfortunately, what begins as <u>temporary</u> relief for stress and anxiety often ends up being a **lifetime of antidepressant** medications. Some people find their miracle medication (Prozac, for example) and it works well for them for years! While others bounce from one medication to the next looking for hope in a bottle. Unfortunately, most of them (long termers) are never able to "kick the antidepressant habit" because the physical withdrawal is devastating...and potentially deadly. Worse yet, over time the medications begin to <u>lose their ability to soften</u>

<u>depression AND they come with serious long-term physical side effects.</u>

Taking a medication that can't fix the problem for the rest of your life make no sense at all.

Children as young as 4 years old are being prescribed anti-depressants today. Some for anxiety and some for depression. It's hard to fathom a 4-year-old suffering from depression. I don't doubt that they do, but I wonder where it comes from?

A 4-year-old doesn't have the reasoning ability to evaluate life circumstances or to process those circumstances into a place of doom and gloom all on their own.

A 4-year-old doesn't conjure up destructive thoughts and they don't know (or shouldn't know) anything about suicide yet. Somebody, somewhere mentioned "hurting yourself" or "killing yourself" – a counselor, parent, school teacher? - young children simply do not come up with the idea of taking their own lives on their own.

Could it be something as simple as diet – a diet filled with sugar, preservatives and every toxic mix known to mankind – could be wreaking havoc on their overall health and their ability to reason and cope? A **poor diet can do more cognitive damage than**

most people could ever imagine! If we prescribe medications FIRST, we'll never find the underlying problem.

If medications are necessary, then they should at least be used with caution. If not, your "temporary" crisis management will turn into a lifetime of medicating with symptoms that will eventually return.

If at all possible, it's best to learn to cope – not "dope".

STEP #1

Admit it - your life is out of control!

Admit that you're in the dark place and that it has taken control over your life…<u>until now</u>. The first and most important step in any "recovery" program is to admit that you are powerless and (in this case) that depression has taken over your life.

Placing blame on people or circumstances for you being in the dark place is NOT the answer to overcoming anything…from alcoholism to depression. You are where you are and it's time to climb out; until you can face your reality and stop placing blame you can't begin to kick your depression to the curb.

It is important to take a realistic look at our lives if we want our lives to be different than they are today AND it's time to stop pointing fingers. Until we do, we can't begin the journey toward freedom from that dark, debilitating place.

All of those "If I had a partner," "I'm all alone," "If I had better friends," "if only my parents," "I hate my job," "I hate my life," serve no good purpose in life…**in or out of depression**.

We <u>ALL</u> wish life could be different in some way at some point. We have the power to change MOST of our circumstances, and for all those we can't change – we have the power to face to face them with courage.

It's a tough pill to swallow when you're in misery, but it's important for you to accept that whatever it is that you're blaming for being in the dark place is just an excuse you use to justify why you're there - and the longer you give the dark place "life"… you'll remain there.

I don't doubt for a minute that you have circumstances that are overwhelming for you…ones that "pushed" you into the dark place. I've been there and done that myself! I'm on the other side of the dark place now, but I did my fair share of making excuses for being there. I was so consumed with the "if only's" that I couldn't find the strength to function. My troubles raced through my mind like a NASCAR track and the more they raced the weaker I became; until finally I settled into the dark place to escape all those things I couldn't cope with.

Life happens to all of us, and sometimes we face circumstances that take us to the breaking point. My journey is different from your journey and yours is different from mine, but every journey is filled with pain and disappointment.   Trust me, you wouldn't want my circumstances and I sure don't want yours! We each get our own unique set of circumstances and we each just one shot at this life.

When you're hidden away in the dark place, you're wasting a precious life and you're losing out on all the good that is possible for you! You're giving it away!

 Isn't it time to enjoy the quality of life that you hear so many other people talk about? It's possible for you to have a quality life of your own! You are no less worthy of good things than anybody else. God didn't decide to make you miserable while the rest of the work is happy! You've just gone to the dark place that has a way of convincing you that good things are not possible for you. Stop believing the lies you tell yourself! I assure you, it IS possible for you to get a handle on that dark place and have a wonderful life of peace…IF you're willing to take the steps to get you there.

Why are some people more capable of coping throughout those trying circumstances while others face anxiety and depression? The simple answer is that we just don't know.

It could be that some people have never learned to cope…. coping IS a process.

It could be that some people have no faith in a "higher power" (I know Him to be "God") that can see them through their circumstances.

It could be that some people are so focused on themselves that they can't handle any disappointments at all!

It could be as simple as the fact that some people have never learned survival techniques to help them rationalize the irrational or to put the right perspective on the challenges.

Believe it or not, it could be a simple as a poor diet! A poor diet (mineral deficiencies) can rock your world and one "symptom" is fatigue and depression! When the body is toxic, the brain isn't far behind and all kinds of cognitive issues can manifest. If you struggle with the dark place and you've not had a good physical work-up in a while, it might be time

Whatever the reason…some people cope…some people don't. If you're prone to go to the dark place as a way of coping like I did, it's time to learn to cope!

First things first. **Admit that you're in the dark place** and that it has had control over you…<u>until now</u> **and determine to FIGHT to climb your way out!**

STEP #2

Today I'm going to GET UP!

Some people crawl into bed and pull the covers over their heads while others take to the couch…wherever it is that you flop - **GET UP!**

Force yourself out of bed even though you tell yourself it isn't possible. You're too tired. You're too weak. You don't feel like it. You're sick. The list of excuses is a mile long. The energy it takes to get up can FEEL overwhelming BUT IT IS NOT impossible…you've just **convinced yourself** it is.

> *God grant me the serenity*
>
> *to accept the things I cannot change;*
>
> *courage to change the things I can;*
>
> *and wisdom to know the difference.*

If you're serious about climbing out of the dark place, then you need to **rewire your brain** – away from those things you tell yourself you can't do - and on to all the things you can. Have the COURAGE to do the things you CAN and the WISDOM to know the difference!

People in the *dark place* almost always get moving for the things they think are too important to miss. Some are able to function at work. Some are able to drive the kids to school. Some get up for the favorite TV show, some manage to make it to the dinner table…but after that…most go crawling back to the dark place as fast as they can get there!

I've not heard of even one depressed person that stayed in bed until they died.

Most don't woller in their own waste…they make it to the bathroom.

Most don't die of dehydration…they find their way to water.

 Most don't die of starvation…they manage to find their way to food AND most of the time it's not just sustenance…they actually have a preference for what they eat.

So, if you can find the energy to take care of your basic human needs, then you can find what it takes to GET UP for the sake of climbing out of the dark place too.

If you're not willing to do Step 1 – there is no reason to move to Step #2.

If that's the case, please pass the book along to someone else.

STEP #3

Today is going to be a GOOD day!

Good days don't just happen for anybody! Do you really think that everybody you encounter is having a much better day that you are just because they're functioning and you're not? Think again!

The people having the best days are the people who EXPECT it to be a good day!

They determine to do their part to make it a great day! They meditate in the mornings and they proclaim a good day <u>before their day even gets going</u>!

Why would you EVER have a good day if you anticipate the worst?

How can you ever climb your way out of the dark place when you spend so much time focusing on how bad your life is and you count all the reasons you have for being miserable?

If you want to climb out of the dark place, then you must BELIEVE that it IS possible, and you must make it a priority to PROCLAIM a good day…**one day at a time.**

The human mind is incredibly complex, but it can be fooled too. When you dwell on the negative - that's exactly what you'll manifest. But when you SPEAK positive words…when you PROCLAIM a good day… when you repeat the positive over and over…**your brain begins to believe it!**

Proclaim it…

TODAY IS GOING TO BE A GOOD DAY!

NOTHING WILL RUIN THIS GOOD DAY FOR ME!

NOTHING STANDS IN THE WAY OF MY HAPPINESS

TODAY I <u>CHOOSE</u> HAPPINESS

You have NO IDEA how empowering it is to rewire your brain! Work your way from the dark place and on to positive things!

Read an inspirational book.

Real the Bible.

Play music that makes you happy and force yourself to sing!

Whatever it is that you need to do to override the negative you've filled yourself up with and replace it with POSITIVE-**just do it!**

Notice I didn't say do it "if you feel like it"– I said DO IT - <u>especially</u> when you don't feel like it!

Today is going to be a good day!

You have the power to make it be!

Will you commit to doing your part to AFFIRM a good day – today and every day?

Climbing out of the dark place is positively possible for you…BUT you have to WANT to be happy and you have to be WILLING to work for it!

Are you?

STEP #4

Filter Your Life!

Garbage in-garbage out!

Life is filled with plenty of negative things that can influence the way that you cope. From the news, to toxic friends, to horrifying TV shows, to books. Whatever you fill yourself up with is what you'll manifest.

 People struggling through the dark place have NO PLACE adding to the challenges by surrounding themselves with things that would darken even the brightest of lights – depression or not! If you want to climb out of the dark place its time to filter your life.

They say that misery loves company, and that's usually true. If you're in the dark place you might be drawn to other people walking through the dark place too - and if you aren't careful, you'll find yourself comparing notes on how miserable life is! What possible good can come out of that? If you're in the dark place, you have NO PLACE spending time with someone in the same boat. There will come a time when you're strong enough to be a good friend to someone else…for now you're only adding insult to injury. You're not strong enough to spend your time with another depressed person! If you can't help yourself, so you sure can't help them, and they'll only drag you down deeper than you already are.

It's easy to understand how you could find yourself hanging around with like-minded people, because **you aren't always easy to be around.** That's sad, but it's often true.

Some people don't understand where you are…they just know they feel uncomfortable being around you because you seem so lifeless.

Some people try to understand what you're feeling but nothing they say seems to help so they quit trying.

Some people think you can be entertained out of the dark place and when none of the activities fix your "mood" they quit bothering.

Some people know what its like to be where you are, and they get impatient when they make suggestions for things that might help you while you make nothing but excuses.

Don't be too hard on your family friends.

Depression isn't easy on anybody…including them!   When you're on the other side of your dark place you'll realize how difficult it must have been for your family and friends to see you so lifeless, not knowing what they could do to help.

Some of you will blame the fact that your friends have abandoned you in your darkest hour, and you'll credit them for a piece of your journey while you're at it. But that's not true. Nobody puts us in the dark place…we do that ourselves.

Nobody is responsible for our happiness…WE are responsible for our own!

Don't worry, one day **all** of your relationships will be rich and full again. But it all comes down to you…. and how hard you're willing to work to climb your way out of the dark place.

One last thing about filtering your life before we move on to the next step…

Lots and lots of people turn to alcohol to numb the pain of their depression A glass of wine here – a tequila there. If you're on antidepressant medications, you **already KNOW you shouldn't be drinking alcohol!** Alcohol is <u>a depressant</u>.

Does it make any sense to you that you would drink a depressant when you're already depressed OR that you'd drink a depressant while you're taking ANTI depressant meds? Seriously?

Stop fooling yourself and pick your poison. If you insist on antidepressants, then stay away from alcohol. If you're not on medication and you're suffering through depression…STAY AWAY FROM ALCOHOL…the last thing you need is something to drive you deeper into the hole you're trying to get out of!

You might be surprised to learn how common it is for alcoholics to suffer with depression, and they began abusing alcohol just to numb the pain. You think you've got problems now? Keep drinking alcohol to number your pain and you just might find yourself in a different kind of 12 Step Program down the line.

It's time to take care of yourself and to make wise decisions that will lead to you climbing out of the dark place and to filter out all those things that could be making matters worse.

Keep filtering!

STEP #5

GET READY…GET SET…GO!

Even if you have nothing to do and no place to go - **GET DRESSED and ready to go as if you do**!

Take a shower.

Wash your hair.

Fight the urge to get back into your pajamas or your sweats!

How can you feel good about your life if you don't even bother with YOU?

Who cares? Well, maybe nobody in your world is complaining about the fact that you don't care about your appearance, but you have no choice if you want to climb out of the dark place! It sounds like it should be low on the list of priorities for you but it's actually a GIANT step in forcing you to feel better about yourself.

You may whine about the "energy" it takes to get yourself into the shower, but if you're honest with yourself afterward you'll confess that you feel much better afterwards! Nothing soothes the soul like a hot shower or a bubble bath!

Don't overthink it…just do it.

If you're a female – put on your make up as if you have someplace special to go. You'll be forced to look in the mirror when you do, and you'll see for yourself that the dark place is showing on your face. Look long and hard and FORCE YOURSELF to say, "you're worth it."

If you're a male – shave your face as if you have someplace special to go. You'll be forced to look at yourself too and when you do…FORCE YOURSELF to say, "you're worth it."

Who cares if you don't believe it at this very moment! When you keep repeating those same words every time you look in the mirror, the most amazing thing will eventually happen; you'll start believing what you say!

You might be having a hard time believing you're worth the effort but there are plenty of people in your life that believe you are. Isn't it time for you to believe it too?

I believe it.

God believes it.

Just lather, rinse, and repeat and before long you will believe it too!

Don't underestimate the therapeutic benefit of getting up, getting showered, putting on your make up or shaving and getting dressed as if you have someplace special to go!

If you want to climb out of the dark place, part of your journey requires that you get your BODY out of the dark place too. Don't worry…before too long your body, mind and SPIRIT will all be on the same page.

Get up.

Get showered.

Get spruced up.

Get dressed.

Tell yourself "I am worth it."

And then, congratulate yourself on a job well done. I KNOW how hard it is to take these steps when you feel overwhelmed with exhaustion. But I ALSO know this is a necessary step to get you in gear for recovery.

One step closer to climbing out of the dark place…

STEP #6

GO OUTSIDE!

There's a whole world waiting for you…it's time to go outside. That's what people in the land of the living do and you need to do it too!

It doesn't matter if its morning, noon or night.

It doesn't matter if the sun is shining or the rain is pouring.

It doesn't matter if its freezing cold or hot as Hades…**GET OUT THERE!**

You are much more connected to nature than you care to admit right now and it's time for you to enjoy its benefits. How will you ever to climb out of the dark place if you insist on living in the dark?

Step outside and look for something beautiful. You can't find something beautiful? Then stay out there until you do! It could be a bird, or a cloud, a flower or anything in between. There's plenty of beauty out there and we're going to nudge you into finding it AND appreciating it again.

Once you find something beautiful, don't rush back inside. Stand there and ponder it. Marvel at its beauty. Consider the

One who made it. Focus on its colors or the way it moves. Think about how long its been since you seen beauty like that. Only when you believe that you could draw a picture of it without looking can you come back inside.

Your visit outside might only be a minute or two in the beginning, but before you know it, you'll be spending longer and longer out there because soon all the beauty will begin to unfold all around you when you're motivated to find it.

Find a comfortable spot to sit. Soak in the sun or howl at the moon!

You have so much to live for and so much left for you to experience in this life.

Begin to trade tiny little pieces of your dark place for the for the bright and beautiful.

Believe me, your soul can't resist nature and your mind will follow suit.

You're making great progress!

STEP #7

So…

You've gotten yourself up.

You've said your affirmations.
You've gotten showered and dressed as if you have some place special to go.

You've gone outside and you've begun to appreciate the world again.

And now it's time to **MOVE YOUR BODY!**

How ironic that the dark place robs us from doing all the things we need to do to climb out of it, and exercise is one of those things. Don't fret. We're not talking marathons…just movement!

Did you know that when you exercise, your body releases chemicals called endorphins, and that the endorphins trigger a positive feeling in the body similar to that of morphine? It's true! That sounds like just what the doctor ordered for depression, but you've got to MOVE to get it!

Don't think about it…just do it!

Start slow. Maybe you take a walk around the block or dance to some of that happy music you've been playing. Maybe you go for a swim or get on that treadmill that is collecting dust. Ride a bike or go to the gym you've been paying for and never use! It doesn't matter how fast and furious you move right now…just MOVE YOUR BODY to get those endorphins going.

While you're moving parts of you that you haven't moved in a while, speak some positive words to yourself. You might as well kill two birds with one stone, right?

I CAN DO THIS

I'M FEELING BETTER EVERY DAY

I AM HAPPY

I AM BLESSED

I AM VICTORIOUS OVER DEPRESSION

Remember, you CAN rewire your brain to focus on beautiful things, but it takes effort to get you there.

So anytime you have time, speak those positive words and

KEEP MOVING!

STEP #8

You're strong enough now to step out into the land of the living - your first step should be to go to a "feel good" place.

Go to church

Go to a synagogue

Go to an uplifting movie

Go hear some of your favorite musicians

As you venture out its important to venture out to things that you know will make you feel good. It's going to take a lot of effort to push yourself out the door, why not make it worth while when you do, right?

As you get up, get showered, get dressed and start moving, don't let yourself slip into negative thoughts about your venture! Since you've been in that dark place, that's exactly what you'll be inclined to do!

Don't think about how tired you are.

Don't think about how long you'll be gone from home.

Don't question whether it will be worth it or not

GET EXCITED

BE PROUD OF YOURSELF FOR GETTING THIS FAR

DETERMINE TO HAVE A FANTASTIC TIME

If you'll be venturing out with company, be sure that you venture out with someone you like spending time with too! People don't exist to make you happy, but for this first big step into the land of the living, you won't want the journey to be with someone argumentative or one that is prone to criticize everything in sight. Pick a positive pal and enjoy the ride.

Once you see what it feels like to get out into the land of the living, you'll soon begin to believe that all the other places you need to go to function in a "normal," light-filled life aren't so hard to do after all.

Have a great time and embrace the life that's just beyond the dark place!

It's your life and you're starting to live it again!

ENJOY IT!

STEP #9

If you're like most people, you probably have some peace to make once you begin to see the light.

Perhaps you need to apologize to your loved ones for unintentionally making their lives miserable while you were lost in the dark place.

Maybe you need to apologize to the ones you blamed for sending you to the dark place in the first place…because now you know that nobody has that power over you no matter what they do!

Is there some forgiving you need to do? We all get wronged and we always will. That's just the way it goes in life. Some wrongs are minor and some we THINK are unforgiveable…but nothing is unforgiveable.

When we extend forgiveness, WE are the ones to win! Withholding forgiveness will only hurt you, and unforgiveness could be exactly what sent you to the dark place in the first place!

If you want to climb out of the dark place, and STAY OUT of the dark place, you need to forgive anybody and everybody that hurt you. It's not optional in your recovery!

When you finally forgive you will feel the most unbelievable weight lifted off your shoulders and it won't take long for you to be walking taller.

Just do it!

Don't forget, if you want to be forgiven for all the things you've done to hurt somebody else…in and out of your depression… then you need to be willing to forgive whoever hurt you too.

Lastly, you might need to forgive yourself. Sometimes we shove ourselves into the dark place all because of things we've done or said, and we just can't forgive ourselves. If you own that nonsense it *will own you*…and until you learn to forgive yourself, you can't climb out of the dark place.

There is nothing that God refuses to forgive.

There's nothing so horrible that would cause Him to stop loving you!

He wants you to celebrate who you are!

He loves you!

You need to love yourself!

When you've got those two things right, it doesn't matter who else loves you!

You know what happens when you realize how much He loves you and then you learn to love yourself again?

You become loveable to everybody around you!

Make your peace.

Let it go.

Forgive.

It's a new beginning for you. Leave the pain behind and determine to have a bright tomorrow!

STEP #10

DO something kind for a stranger

No offense, but when we're in the dark place we are incredibly self-centered. The entire world is revolving around our pain and everybody around us pays the price.

One of the best ways to get away from making your own life the center of attention is to do something for someone else. There's just something about sacrificing for another human being that has a way of transferring the attention away from ourselves and on to someone else. Ironically, the more of ourselves that we give away to someone else, the more fulfilled we are! It's a beautiful thing!

So, do something kind for someone else.

A total stranger…not someone you already know

That's what true sacrifice looks like…to give time, talent or resources to someone we know nothing about!

A simple act of kindness and YOU'RE the one to do it!

And if it's possible…do it in secret…just because you can.

You have no idea how good you'll feel when you meet the need of another human being. You'll feel empowered. You'll feel fulfilled. And more than anything else, you'll feel grateful that you could.

Life isn't about us, but you sure couldn't tell that from the front row seat in the dark place! It's focusing on our own lives and our own set of circumstances that gets us into trouble because that's not the way life is supposed to roll.

Nothing about your journey has ever been about you! It may be your story, but your story is intended to help someone else somewhere down the road.

It's when you step outside of yourself to serve someone else that you begin to see what the journey is all about, and it's that simple act of kindness for a total stranger that will help drive the message home to your heart.

Just imagine how you'll be able to help other people when you get out of the dark place!

It's pretty exciting when you look at it that way!

Great things are just ahead.

You're up…you're moving…and you're paying forward some blessings that only you can give!

You have a whole lot more to live for than you may ever have imagined!

I'm excited for you because *I know* you're about to turn the corner from the focus on yourself and your life to focusing on someone else and their needs.

When you get outside yourself. the entire world opens up and you're back in the driver's seat.

Don't look now but the dark place isn't as dark as it used to be.

Darkness can't reside with the light! Keep shining!

KEEP GIVING to someone else just because you can.

STEP 11

Now that you've made it to the simple act of kindness step, you need to keep going!

You won't be doing a simple act of kindness every once in a while, - you need to LIVE outside yourself by giving to others all the time! Since it's almost impossible to identify individual needs on your own, find a good cause and volunteer for it!

I know you're busy. Everybody's busy. But we all find time for things that are important to us, and you're no different.

Volunteering doesn't mean that you'll spend 20 hours a week – or 10 hours a week – or even 5 hours a week if you don't have the time to dedicate. What's important is that you sign up AND that you keep your commitment to selflessly volunteer just because you can.

Serve in a soup kitchen!

Help at a homeless shelter!

Teach someone to read!

It doesn't matter if it's doing the laundry for a homeless shelter or serving up food to the hungry - just find a worthwhile cause and GIVE of yourself without complaining.

If you want to get out of the dark place, and stay out of the dark place, it is IMPERATIVE that you keep yourself from focusing on your trials and tribulations…they only lead to the dark place all over again.

Make it a habit to volunteer.

Make it your mission to make a difference.

Make sacrificial giving a part of who you are.

And remember, it's the one doing the giving that is blessed ten times more than the one to receive. Give selflessly and celebrate your life!

You're making a difference in the lives of others!

Soon you'll be so far outside of yourself and so far away from the dark place that you'll have trouble even remembering what it felt like!

STEP 12

Lather, rinse, repeat

Once you've fallen into that dark place you'll be inclined to go back there again! Like a rubber band, you stretch your way out and then withdrawal right back to where you came from if you aren't careful! Never let your guard down…EVER.

I don't know why it works that way…it just does.

Consider it your "weak spot" in life.

So, the steps you've taken to climb out of the dark place should be a daily reminder AND a way of life for you for as long as you live.

You won't always need to remind yourself to do the simple things that make the big difference…but you'll always need to live outside your own life and you'll ALWAYS need to have an attitude of gratitude. That's the key to climbing out and staying out of the dark place.

Lather, rinse and repeat and enjoy the light!

CLOSING

I pray these simple steps will serve you well and that you'll find your way out of the dark place soon. If that's the case, please pay it forward to someone else who is stuck in the dark place with no idea how to climb out.

When you're on the other side of the dark place you'll begin to see so many other people around you who are where you were. You'll see it in their eyes. You'll see it in their smile. You'll recognize ALL the signs because you've been there and done that yourself. When you see it, reach out to them and do whatever you can to help them find their way back to the light too. No doubt that's (in part) why you found yourself there…to help someone else…it's not about you.

Lastly, depression is nothing to take lightly and it's not always easy to reach someone lost in the dark. Don't assume they're okay. Don't assume they'd never harm themselves! Hope for the best but prepare for the worst doing everything in your power to reach them. Encourage them to seek professional help and share suicide hotline numbers with them.

Pay it forward. **That's what this life is all about!**

SERENITY PRAYER

God grant me the serenity

to accept the things I cannot change;

courage to change the things I can;

and wisdom to know the difference.

Living one day at a time;

enjoying one moment at a time;

accepting hardships as the

pathway to peace;

taking, as He did, this sinful world

as it is, not as I would have it;

trusting that He will make all things right if I surrender

to His Will;

that I may be reasonably happy in this life

and supremely happy with Him

forever in the next. Amen

PSALM 40:1-3

*I waited patiently for the L*ORD*;*
he turned to me and heard my cry.
He lifted me out of the slimy pit,
out of the mud and mire;
he set my feet on a rock
and gave me a firm place to stand.
*He put a **new song** in my mouth,*
a hymn of praise to our God.

LYNN GARDNER is a trainer, coach and author and friend. She resides on a farm in Northern Virginia and she makes it her mission to serve others in and out of her business! Today she is on a mission to raise the barometer of Faith in the workplace by sharpening the Skills for Success of workplace Believers from all walks of life. Lynn is the proud mother of four children and proud grandmother to four grandchildren, and the legacy of her laughter, love and Faith can be seen in them all.

For more information on soon-to-be-released books or to review our schedule of upcoming events:
info@liquid-assets-usa.com or 202.241.1542

NEW RELEASES IN 2019

Re-Inventing Yourself Over 50

Vaccines…the Cause or the Tipping Point?

New Age of an Age-Old Business!

www.livinglarger.life

lynn@livinglarger.life

202.241.1542

www.ingramcontent.com/pod-product-compliance
Lightning Source LLC
Chambersburg PA
CBHW070827240726
48654CB00007B/503